INTRODUCTION

The term "family meals" is all too frequently associated with plain, unexciting meals. Although busy mothers only have limited time to spend in the kitchen, there are plenty of quick-to-prepare, inexpensive dishes which are just that little bit different and suitable for all the family.

Here you will find a tempting selection of recipes, ranging from tasty versions of well-known favorites, such as hamburgers and savory cauliflower cheese, to more adventurous recipes for chilled soups, pâtés and mouth-watering desserts.

NOTES

Standard spoon and cup measurements are used in all recipes. All spoon and cup measures are level.

Fresh herbs are used unless otherwise stated. If unobtainable substitute a bouquet garni of the equivalent dried herbs, or use dried herbs instead but halve the quantities stated.

Use freshly ground black pepper where pepper is specified.

Ovens should be preheated to the specified temperature.

D0126038

Carrot and Orange Soup

2 tablespoons butter
  or margarine
1 tablespoon oil
1 lb carrots, sliced
2 medium-size
  onions, chopped
3 tablespoons all-
  purpose flour
4 cups chicken stock
  or broth
grated rind and juice
  of ½ orange
juice of ½ lemon
salt and pepper
croûtons for garnish
  (optional)

Heat the butter and oil in a saucepan, add the carrot and onion and sauté until softened. Sprinkle in the flour and cook, stirring, for 1 minute. Remove from the heat and stir in the stock. Return to the heat and bring to a boil, stirring.

Add the orange rind and juice, lemon juice, salt and pepper to taste. Cover and simmer for 30 minutes.

Cool slightly, process in a blender or food processor until smooth. Heat through before serving, with croûtons if desired.

Serves 4 to 6

NOTE: To make croûtons, sauté bread cubes in butter until crisp.

Cold Cucumber Soup

1 large cucumber
2 cups plain yogurt
½ cup sour cream
salt and pepper
1–2 tablespoons
   finely chopped
   mint
mint sprigs for
   garnish

Peel the cucumber and grate
coarsely. Mix with the yogurt, sour
cream and salt and pepper to taste.
Chill for about 2 hours.

   Stir in chopped mint to taste.
Pour into chilled soup bowls and
top with mint sprigs to garnish.
Serves 6

Quick Mushroom Soup

4 tablespoons butter
  or margarine
6 tablespoons all-
  purpose flour
2½ cups chicken
  stock or broth
1¼ cups milk
½ lb mushrooms,
  finely chopped
1 clove garlic,
  crushed (optional)
salt and pepper
1 tablespoon lemon
  juice
1 tablespoon
  chopped parsley
½ cup light cream
paprika for garnish

Melt the butter in a saucepan, then stir in the flour. Cook, stirring, for 1 minute, then gradually stir in the stock and milk. Bring to a boil, stirring constantly.

Add the mushrooms, garlic, if using, salt and pepper to taste and lemon juice. Simmer for 5 minutes, then stir in the parsley and cream. Reheat gently; do not allow to boil. Pour into individual soup bowls and sprinkle with paprika.
Serves 6

Pea and Ham Soup

1 cup (8 oz) split
  peas, rinsed and
  sorted
1 small ham hock
6 cups water
4 tablespoons butter
  or margarine
1 medium-size
  onion, chopped
2 potatoes, cubed
2 stalks celery,
  chopped
salt and pepper

Place the peas and ham hock in a
large saucepan with the water and
bring to a boil. Cover and simmer
for 3 hours.

Melt the butter in a skillet, add
the onion, potato and celery and
sauté until softened.

Remove the ham hock from the
pan, cool slightly, then remove the
meat from the bone, discarding the
fat. Dice the meat and set aside.

Add the sautéed vegetables to the
peas, cover and simmer until all the
vegetables are tender. Cool slightly
and process in a blender or food
processor until smooth.

Return to the pan, add the
reserved ham and salt and pepper to
taste and heat through before serving.
Serves 6 to 8

Vegetable Soup

4 slices bacon, diced
2 medium-size
  onions, chopped
2 large leeks,
  chopped
1 parsnip, chopped
2 carrots, chopped
1 medium-size
  potato, chopped
4 cups beef stock or
  broth
1 can (8 oz)
  tomatoes
2 bay leaves
$\frac{1}{4}$ teaspoon dried
  thyme
1 tablespoon
  chopped parsley
salt and pepper

Sauté the bacon in a skillet. Add the vegetables and cook until they are softened.

Pour in the stock and add the tomatoes with their juice, herbs and salt and pepper to taste. Bring to a boil, cover and simmer for 30 to 45 minutes or until the vegetables are cooked.

Allow the soup to cool a little, then remove the bay leaves. Process in a blender or food processor until smooth. Return to the pan to heat through before serving.

Serves 4 to 6

Leek and Potato Soup

- 4 tablespoons butter or margarine
- 1 tablespoon oil
- 6 leeks, sliced
- 4 medium-size potatoes, sliced
- 5 cups chicken stock or broth
- salt and pepper
- pinch of grated nutmeg
- $\frac{3}{4}$ cup light cream
- chopped chives for garnish (optional)

Heat the butter and oil in a saucepan, add the leeks and sauté for about 10 minutes or until softened. Add the potatoes, stock, salt and pepper to taste, and nutmeg. Cover and simmer for about 30 minutes or until the vegetables are tender. Cool slightly and process in a blender or food processor until smooth.

If the soup is to be served hot, return to the saucepan, add the cream and heat through; do not allow to boil. Adjust the seasoning if necessary.

If serving cold, stir in the cream and chill. Adjust the seasoning and garnish with chopped chives, if desired.

Serves 6

French Onion Soup

4 tablespoons butter
  or margarine
4 large onions,
  sliced
1½ tablespoons all-
  purpose flour
4 cups beef stock or
  broth
salt and pepper
GARNISH:
4–6 slices French
  bread
½ cup shredded sharp
  Cheddar cheese

Melt the butter in a saucepan, add
the onions and sauté until softened
and just beginning to color.
Sprinkle in the flour and cook,
stirring, until lightly browned.
Remove from the heat and
gradually add the stock. Return to
the heat and bring to a boil,
stirring. Add salt and pepper to
taste and simmer for 30 minutes.

Pour into individual ovenproof
bowls and float a slice of French
bread in each. Sprinkle with cheese
and place under a preheated broiler
until golden and bubbling.
Serves 4 to 6

Lettuce Soup

4 tablespoons butter
  or margarine
1 medium-size head
  lettuce, shredded
1 medium-size
  onion, finely
  chopped
2½ cups chicken
  stock or broth
salt and pepper
1 teaspoon sugar
croûtons for garnish
  (see page 6)
BECHAMEL SAUCE:
1¼ cups milk
1 onion
4 cloves
4 peppercorns
pinch of grated
  nutmeg
2 tablespoons butter
  or margarine
4 tablespoons all-
  purpose flour

Melt the butter in a saucepan, add
the lettuce and onion and cook
gently for 10 minutes, stirring
occasionally. Add the stock, salt and
pepper to taste and sugar. Simmer,
covered, for 30 minutes.

Meanwhile, make the sauce. Pour
the milk into a saucepan, add the
onion stuck with the cloves, the
peppercorns and nutmeg. Bring to
a boil slowly, then turn off the heat,
cover and leave for 15 minutes. Strain.

Melt the butter in a small pan
and stir in the flour. Cook, stirring,
for 1 minute, then remove from the
heat and allow to cool. Gradually
add the hot milk, then return to the
heat and bring to a boil, stirring.

Add the sauce to the lettuce,
mixing well, and simmer for
10 minutes. Cool slightly and
process in a blender or food
processor until smooth.

Reheat or, if serving cold, chill.
Adjust the seasoning and garnish
with croûtons.
Serves 4 to 6

Chilled Spanish Tomato Soup

1 lb tomatoes,
  peeled and
  chopped
1 medium-size
  onion, chopped
1 small green
  pepper, seeded
  and chopped
1 clove garlic,
  crushed
1 tablespoon white
  wine vinegar
2 tablespoons olive oil
2 tablespoons lemon
  juice
1 slice white bread,
  crusts removed
1¼ cups chicken
  stock or broth
salt and pepper
GARNISH:
diced cucumber
croûtons (see page 6)

Place all the ingredients in a blender or food processor and process for a few seconds until smooth. Pour into a bowl, cover and chill thoroughly.

Serve the diced cucumber and croûtons as a garnish, in separate dishes.

Serves 4

Hot Clam Appetizer

1 can (6½ oz)
  minced clams,
  drained
1 pkg (8 oz) cream
  cheese, softened
4–5 tablespoons
  mayonnaise
1 small onion,
  grated
2 tablespoons
  chopped chives
1 tablespoon
  Worcestershire
  sauce
hot pepper sauce
paprika
TO SERVE:
cocktail rye bread or
  plain melba
  rounds

Place the clams, cream cheese,
mayonnaise, onion, chives,
Worcestershire sauce and hot
pepper sauce to taste in a mixing
bowl and stir with a fork until well
combined.

Spoon into a small baking dish or
small soufflé dish. Sprinkle the top
with paprika. Bake in a preheated
375°F oven for 20 to 25 minutes or
until puffed. Serve with cocktail rye
bread or melba rounds.

Serves 8

Melon and Grapefruit Appetizer

1 honeydew melon
1 lb tomatoes
½ cucumber
1 can (16 oz)
    grapefruit
    sections, drained
chopped chives
    for garnish
DRESSING:
3 tablespoons lemon
    juice
6 tablespoons
    vegetable oil
salt and pepper

Quarter the melon, remove the seeds and skin, and cut the flesh into cubes. Peel and quarter the tomatoes; cut the quarters in half if they are large. Peel the cucumber and cut into cubes.

Mix together the melon, tomatoes, cucumber and grapefruit in a serving dish.

Shake the dressing ingredients together in a screw-top jar and pour over the salad. Sprinkle with chives and chill for 1 hour.
Serves 6

Deviled Ham Dip

1 pkg (8 oz) cream
    cheese, softened
1 can (4½ oz)
    deviled ham
2 tablespoons
    mayonnaise
2 teaspoons prepared
    horseradish
½ onion, grated
½ teaspoon chili
    powder

Combine the cream cheese, ham, mayonnaise, horseradish, onion and chili powder in a bowl. Stir with a fork until well blended. Spoon into a serving bowl and refrigerate for 1 to 2 hours.

Serve with pitta bread, cut into triangles, or with plain melba rounds.
Serves 8 to 10

Chicken Liver Pâté

½ cup butter or
    margarine
½ lb chicken livers,
    trimmed
1 small onion,
    finely chopped
1 clove garlic,
    crushed
1 tablespoon brandy
    or dry sherry
salt and pepper
grated nutmeg
1 bay leaf

Melt half the butter in a skillet. Add the livers, onion and garlic, cover and cook gently for 5 minutes. Remove from the heat, cool slightly, then add the brandy or sherry, with salt, pepper and nutmeg to taste. Process in a blender or food processor until smooth.

Spoon into a small serving dish and place the bay leaf on top. Melt the remaining 4 tablespoons of butter and pour over the pâté. Chill until firm. Serve with toast.
Serves 4

16

FISH

Mackerel in Horseradish Sauce

4 medium-size
  mackerel, cleaned
  and gutted
2 teaspoons
  cornstarch
3 tablespoons
  horseradish sauce
2 tablespoons lemon
  juice
4 tablespoons dry
  white wine
salt and pepper
cucumber slices for
  garnish (optional)

Place the fish, skin side down, in a greased casserole.

Blend the cornstarch into the horseradish sauce, then gradually add the lemon juice and wine. Season with salt and pepper to taste and pour over the fish. Cover and cook in a preheated 325°F oven for 30 minutes, or until tender.

Garnish with cucumber slices, if desired, before serving.

Serves 4

Cheesy Cod

4 cod steaks
¾ cup grated
  Cheddar cheese
1 teaspoon
  Worcestershire
  sauce
1 tablespoon milk
salt and pepper
parlsey sprigs for
  garnish

Place the cod steaks on a greased broiler and broil on one side for 4 to 5 minutes. Mix the remaining ingredients (except parsley) together, with salt and pepper to taste.

Turn the fish over and spread the uncooked side with the cheese mixture. Broil for about 5 minutes or until the fish is cooked and the topping is golden and bubbling. Garnish with parsley.
Serves 4

Fish and Potato Pie

1 lb cod or haddock
 fillets
salt and pepper
1 tablespoon oil
4 tablespoons butter
 or margarine
1 large onion,
 chopped
1 can (16 oz)
 tomatoes
1 clove garlic,
 crushed (optional)
$\frac{1}{4}$ lb mushrooms,
 sliced
$\frac{1}{2}$ teaspoon dried
 thyme
1 teaspoon sugar
1 lb potatoes, cooked
2 tablespoons milk
2 tablespoons grated
 Cheddar cheese

Place the fish in a saucepan with
enough cold water to cover. Season
to taste with salt and pepper. Bring
to a simmer and cook for
10 minutes.

Meanwhile, heat the oil and
2 tablespoons butter in a skillet, add
the onion and sauté for 5 minutes
or until softened. Stir in the
tomatoes with their juice, garlic, if
using, mushrooms and thyme and
cook for 5 minutes. Add the sugar
and salt and pepper to taste.

Drain the fish, discard all skin
and bones, then flake and add to the
tomato mixture. Transfer to an
ovenproof dish.

Mash the potatoes with the
remaining 2 tablespoons butter and
the milk, and season well. Spread
over the fish mixture. Sprinkle with
the grated cheese and bake in a
preheated 400°F oven for about
20 minutes or until golden on top.
Serves 4

Smoked Fish with Corn

$1\frac{1}{2}$ lb finnan haddie
  or smoked cod
  fillets
2 tablespoons butter
  or margarine
4 tablespoons all-
  purpose flour
$\frac{2}{3}$ cup milk
salt and pepper
1 can (16 oz) whole
  kernel corn,
  drained
$\frac{1}{4}$ cup sour cream
  (optional)
parsley sprigs for
  garnish

Place the fish in a large skillet and
add just enough boiling water to
cover. Simmer, uncovered, for
5 minutes, skimming the surface
occasionally. Remove the fish,
reserving $\frac{2}{3}$ cup of the cooking
liquid. Cut the fish into pieces and
place in a casserole.

Melt the butter in a saucepan and
stir in the flour. Cook, stirring, for
1 minute, then gradually add the
milk and reserved cooking liquid.
Bring to a boil, stirring constantly;
season well with salt and pepper.

Stir in the corn and pour the
sauce over the fish. Cover and cook
in a preheated 350°F oven for
20 minutes.

Just before serving, stir in the
sour cream, if using. Garnish with
parsley and serve accompanied by
boiled potatoes or crusty bread.
Serves 4

21

Kedgeree

1 lb finnan haddie
  or smoked cod
  fillets
2 hard-cooked eggs
½ cup butter or
  margarine
1 cup rice, cooked
1 jar (4 oz) chopped
  pimientos,
  drained
1 tablespoon lemon
  juice
salt and pepper
2 tablespoons light
  cream
2 tablespoons
  chopped parsley
  for garnish

Place the fish in a skillet and add just enough boiling water to cover. Simmer for 10 to 15 minutes, skimming the surface if necessary. Drain and flake the fish. Cut the eggs into small wedges.

Melt the butter in a pan and stir in the rice, fish, pimiento and lemon juice. Season to taste with salt and pepper and mix well. Cook, stirring, over moderate heat until heated through. Remove from the heat and stir in the cream. Fold in the eggs, place in a warmed serving dish and garnish with parsley.
Serves 4

Tuna Fish Cakes

2 large potatoes,
  cooked
2 tablespoons butter
  or margarine
1 can (10 oz) tuna,
  drained and
  flaked
2 tablespoons
  chopped parsley
salt and pepper
2 eggs, beaten
1 cup dry bread
  crumbs
oil for frying
GARNISH:
parsley sprigs
lemon wedges

Mash the potatoes with the butter, then mix in the tuna, parsley, salt and pepper to taste and one beaten egg.

Chill the mixture for 20 minutes, then place on a floured surface and shape into a roll. Cut into 8 slices and shape each into a flat round, about 2½ inches in diameter. Dip each fish cake into the remaining beaten egg, then coat evenly with bread crumbs.

Heat the oil in a skillet, add the fish cakes and fry for 2 to 3 minutes on each side or until golden brown and heated through. Garnish each fish cake with a parsley sprig. Serve with lemon wedges.
Serves 4

Cod with Mushrooms

4 cod steaks
½ lb mushrooms,
    sliced
4 tomatoes, peeled
    and sliced
1 clove garlic,
    crushed (optional)
2 tablespoons dry
    white wine
1 tablespoon lemon
    juice
salt and pepper
chopped parsley for
    garnish

Place the cod steaks in a well
greased casserole. Top with the
mushrooms, tomatoes and garlic, if
using. Pour the wine and lemon
juice over and season well with salt
and pepper.
   Cover with foil and bake in a
preheated 350°F oven for
30 minutes. Garnish with chopped
parsley.
Serves 4

Flounder with Spinach

1½ lb spinach
3 tablespoons light
    cream
2 tablespoons butter
    or margarine
salt and pepper
grated nutmeg
8 small flounder
    fillets
2 tablespoons grated
    Parmesan cheese
tomato wedges for
    garnish

Cook the spinach, with just the
water clinging to the leaves after
washing, until tender. Drain
thoroughly and process in a blender
or food processor, or finely chop.
Mix in the cream and butter.
Season well with salt, pepper and
nutmeg. Place in a greased casserole.
   Roll up the fillets and secure
with toothpicks. Arrange them on
the spinach and sprinkle with the
cheese. Cover and bake in a preheated 350°F oven for 30 minutes.
Garnish with tomato wedges.
Serves 4

Whiting in Oatmeal

4 whiting, cleaned
    and gutted
salt and pepper
⅔ cup oatmeal
2 tablespoons butter
    or margarine
1 tablespoon oil
lemon wedges for
    garnish

Rub the fish with a little salt. Rinse
and dry, then sprinkle with salt and
pepper.
   Coat the fish with the oatmeal
and press on firmly. Heat the butter
and oil in a skillet, add the fish and
fry for about 8 minutes, turning
once. Drain on paper towels and
serve with lemon wedges.
Serves 4

Layered Fish Casserole

4 tablespoons butter
  or margarine
4 slices bacon, diced
2 onions, finely
  chopped
4 tomatoes, peeled
  and chopped
1 clove garlic,
  crushed (optional)
salt and pepper
1 tablespoon
  chopped parsley
4 haddock or cod
  fillets
1 tablespoon lemon
  juice
1 cup soft bread
  crumbs
½ cup grated
  Parmesan cheese

Melt the butter in a skillet. Add the bacon, onion, tomato and garlic, if using, and sauté until the onion is softened. Season to taste with salt and pepper, then place in a well greased casserole and sprinkle with parsley. Arrange the fish on top and sprinkle with lemon juice.

Mix the bread crumbs and cheese together and spoon evenly over the fish. Bake in a preheated 325°F oven for 30 minutes, or until the fish is tender and the topping golden brown.

Serves 4

Baked Fish in Cider

1 onion, finely
  chopped
¼ lb mushrooms,
  chopped
4 halibut or cod
  steaks
1 egg, beaten
3 tablespoons dry
  bread crumbs
2 teaspoons lemon
  juice
salt and pepper
¼ cup hard cider
2 tablespoons butter
  or margarine
chopped parsley for
  garnish (optional)

Place the onion and mushrooms in a casserole.

Dip the fish steaks into the egg and coat with bread crumbs. Arrange on top of the onion and mushrooms and sprinkle with the lemon juice and salt and pepper to taste. Spoon the cider over the fish.

Dot with butter and bake in a preheated 325°F oven for 40 minutes or until tender. Garnish with parsley if desired.

Serves 4

Marinated Beef Kabobs

½ cup Italian
  dressing
1 lb beef cubes for
  kabobs
16 medium-size
  mushrooms
16 cherry tomatoes
16 pearl onions
2 large green
  peppers, seeded
  and cut into
  chunks

Pour the dressing over the meat and stir to coat. Cover and marinate in the refrigerator for several hours. Thread 8 skewers alternating meat, mushroom, tomato, onion and pepper.

Place the skewers on a rack in the broiler. Broil for 6 to 8 minutes, 3 to 4 inches from the heat, turning frequently and brushing with marinade. Serve on a bed of rice.
Serves 4

Swiss Steak

1¼ lb beef round steak, cut into 4 portions
salt and pepper
¼ cup all-purpose flour
3 tablespoons oil
2 large onions, chopped
1 pkg (8 oz) beef gravy mix
1 tablespoon prepared brown mustard
parsley sprigs for garnish

Season the meat with salt and pepper and dredge in flour. Heat the oil in a skillet and brown the meat well on both sides. Add the onions and cook until softened. Transfer to a 1 quart casserole.

Prepare the gravy according to the package directions. Add the mustard and pour over the meat. Cover and cook in preheated 350°F oven for 1½ to 2 hours or until the meat is tender.

Garnish with parsley and serve with mashed potatoes.
Serves 4

Spaghetti Bolognaise

BOLOGNAISE
  SAUCE:
2 tablespoons butter
  or margarine
2 tablespoons oil
2 medium-size
  onions, chopped
1 lb lean ground
  beef
$\frac{1}{2}$ lb mushrooms,
  chopped
1 can (16 oz)
  tomatoes
2 cloves garlic,
  crushed
$\frac{1}{2}$ teaspoon dried
  oregano
$\frac{1}{4}$ cup tomato paste
$\frac{2}{3}$ cup beef stock or
  red wine
salt and pepper
SPAGHETTI:
$\frac{3}{4}$ lb spaghetti
2 tablespoons butter
  or margarine
grated nutmeg
GARNISH:
grated Parmesan
  cheese

To make the bolognaise sauce. Heat the butter and oil in a saucepan, add the onions and sauté until softened. Add the meat and cook until evenly browned, stirring to break up the meat. Drain off all the excess fat, then add the remaining sauce ingredients, with salt and pepper to taste.

Bring to a simmering, stirring, then cover and simmer over low heat for 1 hour, adding more liquid if necessary.

Cook the spaghetti in boiling salted water according to package directions and drain thoroughly. Melt the butter in the saucepan, return the spaghetti to the pan and toss well. Season to taste with nutmeg and pepper.

Turn into a serving dish, top with the Bolognaise sauce and sprinkle with Parmesan cheese.
Serves 4

Irish Stew

2 lb lamb for stew,
  cut into cubes
salt and pepper
3 large onions,
  sliced
2 lb potatoes, sliced
2 tablespoons
  Worcestershire
  sauce

Trim any excess fat from the lamb and arrange in a layer in a flameproof casserole. Sprinkle with salt and pepper. Cover with a layer of onions and then potatoes. Repeat until all onions and potatoes have been used.

Sprinkle the Worcestershire sauce over the top, then pour in enough water to come almost to the top layer of potato. Bring to a boil, cover and cook in a preheated 325°F oven for $2\frac{1}{2}$ hours.
Serves 4 to 6

Beef, Pepper and Mushroom Casserole

2 lb beef for stew
3 tablespoons all-
    purpose flour
salt and pepper
3 tablespoons oil
3 medium-size
    onions, chopped
1 large green
    pepper, seeded
    and chopped
2½ cups beef stock
    (or a mixture of
    stock and red
    wine)
1 bouquet garni
½ lb mushrooms,
    sliced

Cut the meat into 1 inch cubes. Season the flour with salt and pepper and use to coat the meat.

Heat the oil in a flameproof casserole, add the meat in batches and quickly brown on all sides. Remove from the casserole.

Add the onion and green pepper to the casserole and sauté until softened. Return the meat to the casserole, sprinkle in any remaining seasoned flour and cook, stirring, for 1 minute.

Gradually add the stock (or stock and wine) and bring to a boil, stirring constantly. Add the bouquet garni, cover and cook in a preheated 325°F oven for 2 hours.

Add the mushrooms, adjust the seasoning if necessary and cook for 30 minutes longer. Remove the bouquet garni. Serve with potatoes and a green vegetable.

Serves 4 to 6

Braised Oxtail

2 oxtails (about
    4 lb), cut into
    2 inch lengths
4 tablespoons beef
    drippings or oil
4 medium-size
    onions, chopped
4 carrots, sliced
3 stalks celery,
    chopped
1 small turnip, diced
2 tablespoons all-
    purpose flour
3 cups beef stock or
    broth
salt and pepper
grated nutmeg
1 bouquet garni
1 bay leaf

Trim any excess fat from the oxtail. Heat the drippings in a large flameproof casserole, add the oxtail and quickly brown on all sides. Remove from the casserole.

Add the vegetables to the casserole and sauté until softened. Sprinkle in the flour and cook, stirring, until the flour is beginning to brown. Gradually add the stock and bring to a boil, stirring constantly.

Return the oxtail to the casserole, season well with salt, pepper and nutmeg, and add the bouquet garni and bay leaf. Cook in a preheated 300°F oven for 4 hours, adding a little more stock or water if necessary.

Remove from the oven, allow to cool and store in the refrigerator overnight. To serve, discard all the fat that has solidified on top of the casserole and simmer gently for 30 minutes. Remove the bouquet garni and bay leaf. Serve with mashed potatoes.
Serves 6

Winter Family Casserole

1 lb beef for stew
3 tablespoons oil
4 tablespoons all-
  purpose flour
3 cups beef stock or
  broth
4 onions, chopped
½ lb carrots, sliced
1 turnip, diced
salt and pepper
grated nutmeg
2 bay leaves
4 medium-size
  potatoes, sliced

Cut the meat into 1 inch cubes. Heat the oil in a flameproof casserole, add the meat a little at a time and quickly brown on all sides, moving the meat cubes to the side of the casserole as they brown.

Sprinkle in the flour and cook, stirring, for 1 minute. Gradually add the stock and bring to a boil, stirring constantly. Lower the heat to simmer and add the onion, carrot and turnip.

Season to taste with salt, pepper and nutmeg and add the bay leaves. Cover and cook in a preheated 325°F oven for 1½ hours.

Add the potatoes and return to the oven for 1 hour. Remove the bay leaves before serving.
Serves 4

Shepherds' Pie

4 large potatoes,
  cooked
2 tablespoons milk
2 tablespoons butter
  or margarine
salt and pepper
1 lb cooked beef or
  lamb
2 medium-size
  onions
1 clove garlic
1¼ cups beef stock or
  broth
1 tablespoon
  Worcestershire
  sauce
½ teaspoon dried
  thyme
½ teaspoon dried
  marjoram
1 tablespoon corn-
  starch dissolved in
  2 tablespoons water

Mash the poatoes with the milk and butter and season to taste with salt and pepper.

Grind the meat, onions and garlic together. Place in a shallow flameproof casserole and add the stock, Worcestershire sauce, herbs and dissolved cornstarch. Add salt and pepper to taste and mix well. Bring to a boil, stirring, and cook, stirring, for 1 minute. Cover and simmer for 15 minutes.

Spread the potato over the meat mixture and broil until the top is crisp and golden brown. Serve with a green vegetable.
Serves 4

Liver and Tomato Casserole

2 tablespoons butter
  or margarine
1 tablespoon oil
2 medium-size
  onions, chopped
1 small green
  pepper, seeded
  and chopped
3 tablespoons all-
  purpose flour
salt and pepper
1 lb beef liver
8 slices bacon, diced
1 can (16 oz)
  tomatoes
4 tablespoons dry
  red wine or water
1 tablespoon
  Worcestershire
  sauce
chopped parsley for
  garnish (optional)

Heat the butter and oil in a flameproof casserole, add the onion and green pepper and sauté until softened.

Season the flour with salt and pepper and use to coat the liver. Add to the pan with the bacon. Increase the heat slightly and brown the liver on both sides. Drain off any excess fat, then stir in the remaining ingredients.

Cover and cook in a preheated 350°F oven for 30 minutes. Garnish with a little chopped parsley, if desired.
Serves 4

Meat Pancakes

1 cup buttermilk
  baking mix
1 egg, beaten
¾ cup milk
salt and pepper
1–1½ cups finely
  diced cooked lamb
1 small onion,
  finely chopped
butter or margarine
  for frying
parsley sprigs for
  garnish (optional)

Place the baking mix in a mixing bowl. Add the egg, milk and salt and pepper to taste. Beat until the pancake mixture is almost smooth. Stir in the meat and onion.

Grease a 7 inch skillet with butter. Pour in enough pancake mixture to cover the bottom of the pan. Cook until the underside is golden, then turn and cook the other side.

Repeat with the remaining mixture to make 6 to 8 pancakes, re-greasing the pan each time. Serve immediately, or stack them on a plate, with a piece of waxed paper between each one, and keep warm in the oven. Garnish with parsley, if desired.

Serves 3 to 4

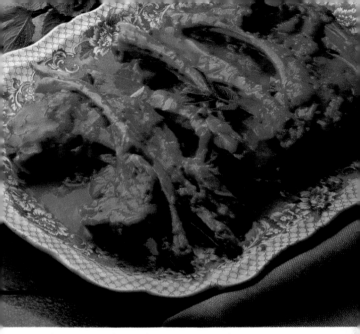

Rib Lamb Chops with Tomatoes and Mint

8 rib lamb chops
2 tablespoons oil
2 medium-size
    onions, chopped
salt and pepper
1 can (16 oz)
    tomatoes, chopped
½ cup chicken stock
    or broth
1 teaspoon sugar
1 tablespoon
    concentrated mint
    sauce
mint sprig to garnish
    (optional)

Place the lamb chops on a rack in the broiler and broil for 5 to 6 minutes per side.

Meanwhile prepare the sauce. Heat the oil in a saucepan. Add the onions and cook until softened. Sprinkle with salt and pepper to taste.

Add the tomatoes with their juice and the stock to the saucepan and stir well. Add the sugar and mint sauce. Bring the mixture to a boil. Lower the heat and simmer for 5 minutes.

Arrange the lamb chops on a warmed serving platter and pour the sauce over. Garnish with a mint sprig, if desired.
Serves 4

Mustard-Glazed Picnic Shoulder

1 5–6 lb smoked
    picnic shoulder
2 tablespoons
    Dijon-style
    mustard
1 cup firmly packed
    brown sugar
$\frac{1}{2}$ cup honey
$\frac{1}{4}$ cup orange juice

Cover the ham with cold water and let soak for 3 to 4 hours. Drain and place the ham in a roasting pan. Bake in a preheated 325°F oven for 1$\frac{1}{2}$ hours.

Prepare the glaze. Combine the mustard, brown sugar, honey and orange juice in a saucepan. Cook over low heat, stirring constantly, until the sugar dissolves.

Remove the ham from the oven and score the top. Spoon the glaze over, return to the oven and bake for 40 to 50 minutes longer, basting the ham occasionally. Serve with pan-roasted potatoes and peas if desired.
Serves 6

Pork in Applejack

$\frac{1}{2}$ lb bacon, diced
1$\frac{1}{2}$ lb pork for stew,
    cubed
salt and pepper
1 lb tart apples,
    peeled, cored and
    sliced
3 medium-sized
    onions, sliced
4 large potatoes,
    thickly sliced
$\frac{2}{3}$ cup applejack
1–1$\frac{1}{4}$ cups beef stock
    or broth
2 tablespoons butter
    or margarine

Cook the bacon in a skillet. Remove from the skillet with a slotted spoon and place in a casserole.

Add the pork cubes to the skillet and sauté until browned on all sides. Remove from the skillet with a slotted spoon and place in the casserole. Season well with salt and pepper.

Arrange the apples and onions over the meat, then top with the potato slices. Pour in the applejack and just enough beef stock to come up to the potato. Sprinkle with salt and pepper, cover and cook in a preheated 350°F oven for 1 hour.

Remove the cover and dot the potato with butter. Increase the heat to 400°F and cook, uncovered, for 30 minutes, or until golden brown.
Serves 4

Kidney Beans and Ham

1 cup cubed cooked
   ham
1 can (15 oz) red
   kidney beans,
   drained
$\frac{1}{2}$ cup ketchup
$\frac{1}{4}$ cup maple syrup
1 medium-size
   onion, chopped
1 tablespoon cider
   vinegar
1 teaspoon dry
   mustard
$\frac{1}{4}$ teaspoon ground
   cloves
salt and pepper

Combine all the ingredients in a
casserole, adding salt and pepper to
taste. Mix well to combine.

Bake, uncovered, in a preheated
350°F oven for 30 minutes or until
hot and bubbly.

Serves 4

Southern-Fried Chicken

flour for coating
salt and pepper
1 tablespoon grated
  nutmeg
1 2½–3 lb
  broiler/fryer, cut
  up
½ cup milk
oil for frying
parsley sprigs for
  garnish

Season the flour with a little salt, a generous amount of pepper and the nutmeg. Dip the chicken pieces into the milk, then coat thoroughly with flour. Dip into the milk again, then coat again with flour.

Pour oil into a deep skillet to a depth of about 1 inch. Heat the oil, then add the chicken pieces and cook for 20 minutes, turning once. Drain well. Garnish with parsley and serve hot or cold with a salad.
Serves 4

Chicken Pie

4 tablespoons butter
or margarine
6 tablespoons all-
purpose flour
$\frac{2}{3}$ cup milk
$1\frac{1}{4}$ cups chicken
stock or broth
3 cups diced, cooked
chicken
$\frac{1}{4}$ lb mushrooms,
chopped
$\frac{1}{2}$ green pepper,
seeded and
chopped
1 tablespoon
chopped parsley
$\frac{1}{2}$ teaspoon celery
salt
salt and pepper
1 5 × 10 inch sheet
($\frac{1}{4}$ of a $17\frac{1}{4}$ oz
pkg) frozen puff
pastry, thawed
beaten egg for glaze

Melt the butter in a saucepan and stir in the flour. Cook, stirring, for 1 minute. Gradually add the milk and stock and bring to a boil, stirring constantly. Stir in the chicken, mushrooms, green pepper and parsley. Season with the celery salt and salt and pepper to taste. Transfer to a $1\frac{1}{2}$ quart casserole.

Roll out the dough to 1 inch larger than the dish. Cut off a $\frac{1}{2}$ inch strip all round and place on the dampened edge of the dish. Moisten the strip with water, then cover with the dough, pressing down firmly.

Trim and flute the edge and vent the crust. Decorate with leaves made from the dough trimmings, if desired, then brush with beaten egg.

Bake in a preheated 425°F oven for 30 minutes or until golden.
Serves 4 to 6

Orange-Baked Chicken

2 large oranges
4 tablespoons butter
    or margarine
1 tablespoon oil
1 2½–3 lb broiler/
    fryer, cut up
2 medium-size
    onions, finely
    chopped
2 tablespoons
    Worcestershire
    sauce
2 tablespoons water
1 tablespoon tomato
    paste
salt and pepper

Thinly peel the rind from 1 orange and cut the rind into thin strips. Grate the rind from the other orange, and squeeze the juice from both oranges.

Heat the butter and oil in a skillet, add the chicken pieces and brown on both sides. Remove from the pan and place in a casserole. Add the onion to the skillet and cook gently for 5 minutes.

Drain off any fat from the skillet, then add the Worcestershire sauce, water, tomato paste, orange rind (strips and grated) and juice. Bring to a boil and season lightly with salt and pepper.

Spoon the sauce over the chicken. Cover and bake in a preheated 350°F oven for 1 hour.

To serve, transfer the chicken to a warmed serving platter and spoon the juices over. Serve with baked potatoes.
Serves 4

Mustard-Glazed Chicken

1 2½–3 lb broiler/
    fryer, cut up
2 tablespoons
    Dijon-style
    mustard
2 tablespoons
    prepared English
    mustard
¼ cup sugar
4 tablespoons lemon
    juice
2 tablespoons oil
2 teaspoons
    Worcestershire
    sauce
salt and pepper
lettuce leaves to serve

Arrange the chicken pieces in a broiler. Put the remaining ingredients, with salt and pepper to taste, in a bowl. Mix well.

Spoon about one quarter of the glaze over the chicken and broil for 15 minutes, spooning over more glaze halfway through cooking. Turn the chicken pieces over, glaze with more mustard mixture and cook for 15 to 30 minutes or until tender, spooning over the remaining glaze during cooking.

Serve on a bed of lettuce.
Serves 4

Chicken and Raisin Casserole

½ cup all-purpose
  flour
salt and pepper
grated nutmeg
1 2½–3 lb
  broiler/fryer, cut
  up
½ cup butter or
  margarine
2 tablespoons oil
2 medium-size
  onions, chopped
4 slices bacon, diced
2½ cups chicken
  stock or broth
½ lb mushrooms,
  sliced
4 medium-size
  tomatoes, peeled
  and chopped
¾ cup golden raisins

Season the flour with salt, pepper
and nutmeg to taste and use to coat
the chicken pieces.

Heat the butter and oil in a
skillet, add the chicken and cook,
turning frequently, for about
10 minutes or until golden brown all
over. Remove from the skillet and
place in a casserole.

Add the onion and bacon to the
skillet and cook until the onion is
softened. Sprinkle in any remaining
seasoned flour and cook, stirring,
for 1 minute. Gradually add the
stock and bring to a boil, stirring.

Pour over the chicken in the
casserole. Add the mushrooms,
tomatoes and raisins. Cover and
cook in a preheated 350°F oven for
1 hour or until tender.
Serves 4

VEGETABLES & SALADS

Zucchini with Tomatoes

4 tablespoons butter
   or margarine
2 tablespoons olive
   or cooking oil
4 medium-size
   zucchini, sliced
4 large tomatoes,
   chopped
2 cloves garlic,
   crushed (optional)
salt and pepper

Heat the butter and oil in a large skillet and sauté the zucchini slices on one side until golden brown. Turn them over and add the tomatoes to the pan just as the zucchini are beginning to brown on the second side. Mix well, add the garlic, if using, season to taste with salt and pepper and continue cooking until the tomatoes are tender. This dish is delicious served with broiled meat.
Serves 4

Glazed Carrots

1 lb carrots
salt
1 chicken or beef
   bouillon cube
1 tablespoon sugar
4 tablespoons butter
   or margarine
chopped parsley for
   garnish (optional)

Leave the carrots whole if small and tender, otherwise slice into rings. Put into a saucepan with just enough lightly salted water to come up to the level of the carrots. Bring to a boil and add the remaining ingredients. Cover and cook for about 20 minutes, then remove the cover and continue cooking for a further 10 to 15 minutes or until the carrots are cooked and the water has nearly boiled away. Drain and serve sprinkled with parsley if desired.

Serves 4

Savory Cauliflower Cheese

1 head cauliflower,
   cut into flowerets
salt and pepper
6 tablespoons butter
   or margarine
2 medium-size
   onions, chopped
4 slices bacon, diced
4 tablespoons all-
   purpose flour
$1\frac{1}{4}$ cups milk
1 cup grated
   Cheddar cheese
1 tablespoon oil
$\frac{1}{4}$ lb mushrooms,
   chopped

Cook the cauliflower in boiling
salted water for 10 to 15 minutes
until tender. Drain thoroughly.

Melt 3 tablespoons of the butter
in a saucepan, add the onion and
bacon and sauté gently for 5 minutes.
Stir in the flour and cook, stirring,
for 1 minute. Gradually stir in the
milk and bring to a boil, stirring.
Cook, stirring, for 2 minutes.
Remove from the heat and add
all but 1 tablespoon of the cheese.

Meanwhile, heat the remaining
butter and the oil in a skillet, add
the mushrooms and sauté over
fairly high heat. Remove from the
pan with a slotted spoon, and stir
into the cheese sauce. Season with
salt and pepper to taste.

Arrange the cauliflower in a
warmed flameproof dish and pour
the sauce over the top. Sprinkle
with the reserved 1 tablespoon of
cheese and broil until golden.
Serves 4

Stuffed Zucchini

2–3 large zucchini
1 tablespoon oil
4 tablespoons butter
or margarine
1 medium-size
onion, finely
chopped
4 slices bacon, diced
1 clove garlic,
crushed (optional)
$\frac{1}{2}$ lb lean ground
beef
$\frac{1}{4}$ cup soft bread
crumbs
2 tomatoes, peeled
and chopped
$\frac{1}{2}$ teaspoon mixed
dried herbs
salt and pepper
grated nutmeg

Peel the zucchini, cut the flesh into
2 inch rounds and remove the seeds.
Place upright in a well greased
large ovenproof dish.

Heat the oil and 2 tablespoons of
the butter in a skillet, add the
onion, bacon and garlic, if using,
and sauté gently until softened. Add
the beef, increase the heat and cook
until browned. Drain off any excess
fat, then mix in the bread crumbs,
tomatoes and herbs. Season well
with salt and pepper.

Sprinkle the zucchini rings with
salt, pepper and nutmeg, then fill
with the stuffing. Dot with the
remaining 2 tablespoons of butter,
cover with foil and bake in a
preheated 350°F oven for 35 to 45
minutes or until the rings are
tender. Serve with crusty French
bread.
Serves 4

Potatoes with Onions

2 beef bouillon cubes
4 medium-size
  onions, thinly
  sliced into rings
salt and pepper
4–6 medium-size
  potatoes, cut into
  $\frac{1}{4}$ inch slices

Crumble the beef cubes into a flameproof casserole. Add 1 inch of water. Heat and stir until the cubes are dissolved.

Arrange the onion rings in the bottom of the dish and sprinkle with pepper and a little salt.

Arrange the potato slices on top, season again, cover and simmer over a low heat for 20 to 30 minutes until the vegetables are tender.

This Australian dish is delicious served as a snack with crusty bread, or as an accompaniment to roast beef.

Serves 4

Creamed Cauliflower

1 head cauliflower,
  cut into flowerets
salt and pepper
2 tablespoons butter
  or margarine
4 tablespoons all-
  purpose flour
1$\frac{1}{4}$ cups milk
grated nutmeg

Cook the cauliflower flowerets in lightly salted boiling water for about 10 to 15 minutes, or until tender. Drain well.

Meanwhile, melt the butter in a small pan and stir in the flour. Cook, stirring, for 1 minute, then gradually stir in the milk. Bring to a boil, stirring constantly, then season to taste with salt, pepper and nutmeg. Cook, stirring, for 2 minutes.

Return the cauliflower to the saucepan and mash with a potato masher or a wooden spoon. Pour in the white sauce and beat until smooth. Spoon into a warmed vegetable dish and sprinkle with a little more nutmeg.

Serves 4

Buttered Leeks with Nutmeg

6–8 leeks, washed
  thoroughly and
  sliced
salt and pepper
4 tablespoons butter
  or margarine
grated nutmeg

Cook the leeks in a pan of
boiling salted water for 10 minutes.
Drain well. Melt the butter in the
saucepan and return the leeks to the
pan. Toss well and sprinkle with
plenty of nutmeg and pepper.
Serves 4

Rutabaga with Bacon

1 medium-size
  rutabaga, cut into
  1 inch cubes
salt and pepper
4 slices bacon, diced
2 tablespoons butter
  or margarine
grated nutmeg
2 tablespoons milk
  or light cream

Cook the rutabaga in boiling salted
water for about 30 minutes or until
tender. Drain thoroughly.

Meanwhile, fry the bacon until
crisp.

Return the rutabaga to the
saucepan and mash to a pulp. Stir in
the butter and bacon and season
with plenty of freshly ground
pepper and nutmeg. Stir in the milk
or cream and heat through. This
dish is delicious with roast pork.
Serves 4

Potato Pancakes

2 eggs, beaten
salt and pepper
2 tablespoons
 chopped parsley
4 medium-size
 potatoes, grated
1 small onion,
 grated (optional)
$\frac{1}{2}$ cup shredded
 Cheddar cheese
 (optional)
oil for frying

Season the beaten egg with plenty
of salt and freshly ground pepper
and add the parsley. Drain any
liquid from the potato and stir into
the egg mixture. Add the onion and
cheese, if using.

Heat a little oil in a skillet, then
place about 2 tablespoons of the
potato mixture in the pan. Flatten
slightly to form a pancake and cook
for about 4 minutes on each side, or
until golden brown.

Transfer to a warmed serving
dish and keep hot. Repeat with the
remaining mixture. Serve with
apple sauce, if desired.
Makes 6 to 8

Grape and Orange Salad with Ham

2 large oranges
1 head lettuce
½ cucumber, peeled
  and diced
1 green pepper,
  seeded and
  chopped
½ lb seedless grapes
4 slices cooked ham
⅔ cup French
  dressing (see page
  57)

Using a serrated knife, peel the oranges, removing all the pith. Cut each segment into 3 or 4 pieces.

Line a salad bowl with a layer of lettuce leaves and arrange a layer of orange, cucumber, pepper and grapes on top. Repeat the layers until all these ingredients are used up.

Roll up the ham slices and arrange on top of the salad. Serve French dressing separately.
Serves 4

Cabbage, Carrot and Apple Salad

2 crisp eating apples
juice of 1 lemon
½ head cabbage,
  shredded
½ lb shredded carrots
½ teaspoon dried
  oregano
⅔ cup French
  dressing (see page
  57)

Peel and thinly slice the apples and coat thoroughly with the lemon juice. Place in a salad bowl with the cabbage and carrot and mix well.

Add the oregano to the French dressing, pour over the salad and toss thoroughly.
Serves 4

Tomato and Cucumber Salad

6–8 tomatoes, sliced
½–1 cucumber,
  peeled and thinly
  sliced
salt and pepper
1 teaspoon sugar
⅔ cup French
  dressing (see page
  57)
½ teaspoon dried
  marjoram

Arrange the tomato and cucumber slices in a shallow serving dish and sprinkle with salt and pepper to taste and the sugar. Let stand for at least 10 minutes.

Pour over the French dressing and sprinkle with the marjoram. Serve immediately. This salad makes a delicious side dish to broiled meats and pasta dishes.
Serves 4

Warm Potato Salad

4 medium-size
    potatoes, cooked
3 hard-cooked eggs
2 medium-size
    onions, chopped
1 small green
    pepper, seeded
    and finely
    chopped
1–2 tablespoons
    chopped chives
1 tablespoon
    chopped parsley
1½ tablespoons cider
    vinegar or lemon
    juice
1 clove garlic,
    crushed (optional)
1 teaspoon
    horseradish sauce
freshly ground black
    pepper

Dice the potatoes and eggs while
still warm. Place in a serving bowl
and add the remaining ingredients,
with pepper to taste. Toss lightly.

Serve immediately, with
mayonnaise, as an accompaniment
to cold beef, pork or ham.

Serves 4

Rice Salad

1 cup rice, cooked
  and drained
  thoroughly
1 green pepper,
  seeded and
  chopped
½ lb tomatoes,
  peeled and
  chopped
1 can (16 oz) whole
  kernel corn,
  drained
2 tablespoons golden
  raisins
1 small onion,
  finely chopped
2 stalks celery,
  finely chopped
2 tablespoons
  chopped parsley
French dressing (see
  page 57)
salt and pepper

Mix together the rice, green
pepper, tomatoes, corn, raisins,
onion, celery and parsley in a large
bowl. Add enough French dressing
to moisten the mixture and season
to taste with salt and pepper. Serve
with cold chicken or ham.
Serves 4

Cauliflower, Mushroom and Onion Salad

½ lb mushrooms,
  thinly sliced
juice of 1 lemon
1 small head
  cauliflower, cut
  into flowerets
2 onions, finely
  chopped
salt and pepper
1–2 tablespoons
  olive oil
⅔ cup French
  dressing (see page
  57)
paprika for garnish

Sprinkle the mushrooms with the lemon juice and put into a salad bowl with the cauliflower and onion. Season to taste with salt and pepper.

Add the olive oil to the French dressing and pour over the vegetables. Marinate for 30 minutes, stirring occasionally.

Just before serving, sprinkle with paprika. This salad is delicious with fish.

Serves 4

French Dressing

1¾ cups olive oil or
    pure corn oil
6 tablespoons red or
    white wine
    vinegar, or ¼ cup
    wine vinegar and
    2 tablespoons
    lemon juice
¾ teaspoon salt
freshly ground
    black pepper to
    taste
1½ teaspoons sugar
    (or to taste)
2 cloves garlic,
    crushed
1 teaspoon Dijon-
    style mustard

Place all the ingredients in a bowl
and beat together thoroughly with
a whisk.

Alternatively, place the ingredients
in a screw-top jar and shake
vigorously. Always give a final
mix immediately before serving.

Makes approximately 2 cups

SUPPERS & SNACKS

Tomato and Cheese Savories

4 pieces pitta bread
4 tablespoons tomato
  sauce
1 lb tomatoes, thinly
  sliced
$\frac{1}{4}$ lb mushrooms,
  thinly sliced
$\frac{1}{2}$–1 teaspoon garlic
  salt
$\frac{1}{2}$–1 teaspoon dried
  marjoram
$\frac{1}{2}$–1 teaspoon dried
  basil
salt and pepper
1 cup grated
  Cheddar cheese

Spread the bread thinly with
tomato sauce, then cover with
tomato and mushroom slices.
Sprinkle with the garlic salt, herbs
and salt and pepper to taste. Top
with the grated cheese.

Place on a greased baking sheet
and bake in a preheated 400°F oven
for 15 minutes, or until the cheese
has melted and the bread is heated
through.
Serves 4

Hamburgers

1 lb lean ground
  beef
1 small onion,
  minced or grated
1 egg, beaten
½ teaspoon dried
  mixed herbs
1 teaspoon
  Worcestershire
  sauce
salt and pepper
4 tablespoons butter
  or margarine
1 tomato, sliced
4 hamburger buns

Place the meat in a bowl and add
the onion, egg, herbs,
Worcestershire sauce and salt and
pepper to taste. Stir well and shape
into 4 hamburgers.

Melt the butter in a skillet, add
the hamburgers and cook for about
4 to 8 minutes, depending on the
degree of doneness desired, turning
once.

Sauté the tomato slices if desired.
Top each hamburger with a slice of
tomato and place on a hamburger
bun. Serve with salad and French
fries.

Makes 4

Onion, Cheese and Egg Bake

4 onions, chopped
4 tablespoons butter
  or margarine
1 green pepper, seeded
  and chopped
2½ cups shredded
  Cheddar cheese
6 eggs
6 tablespoons milk
2 tablespoons
  Worcestershire
  sauce
salt and pepper

Sauté the onions in the butter until softened. Place half the onions in a quiche pan. Sprinkle with half the chopped pepper, then half the cheese. Repeat the layers.

Beat the remaining ingredients together, with salt and pepper to taste, pour into the quiche pan and cook in a preheated 350°F oven for 30 minutes. Serve with crusty bread.

Serves 4

Savory Leek Quiche

BASIC PIE CRUST:
1½ cups all-purpose
  flour
½ teaspoon salt
3 tablespoons butter
  or margarine
3 tablespoons
  shortening
2–3 tablespoons ice
  water
FILLING:
1 lb leeks, washed
  thoroughly and
  sliced
2 tablespoons butter
  or margarine
2 tablespoons all-
  purpose flour
1¼ cups milk
½ teaspoon prepared
  mustard
salt and pepper
¼ lb sliced salami or
  garlic sausage
½ cup shredded
  Cheddar cheese

Sift the flour and salt into a bowl. Cut in the butter and shortening until the mixture resembles coarse crumbs. Add 1 tablespoon water at a time; mix with a fork. Gather into a ball, cover and chill for 30 minutes.

Roll out and use to line an 8 inch quiche pan. Prick the pie shell, line with foil and fill with rice. Bake in a preheated 400°F oven for 10 minutes.

Meanwhile, prepare the filling. Cook the leeks in boiling salted water for about 7 minutes. Drain, cool, then place in the pie shell.

Melt the butter in a small pan, add the flour and cook, stirring, for 1 minute. Remove from the heat and gradually stir in the milk. Bring to a boil, stirring, then simmer for 2 minutes until thick and smooth. Add the mustard and salt and pepper to taste. Cool slightly, then pour over the leeks. Arrange the salami or garlic sausage on top and sprinkle with the cheese.

Return to the oven for about 15 minutes or until the cheese is melted. Serve hot or cold with salad.

Serves 4 to 6

Quick Pepperoni Pizza

1 1 lb loaf frozen
    white bread
    dough
4 tablespoons butter
    or margarine
1 large onion,
    chopped
1 small green
    pepper, seeded
    and chopped
$\frac{1}{2}$ lb pepperoni
$\frac{1}{2}$ teaspoon dried
    mixed herbs
    (optional)

Thaw the dough according to the package directions. Roll or pat out to a 9 or 10 inch round and place on a greased baking sheet. Fold up the edges of the dough to make a rim. Chill in the refrigerator while preparing the topping.

Melt the butter in a skillet, add the onion and green pepper and sauté until the onion begins to brown. Cut the pepperoni into thin strips and mix with the onion and pepper. Spread evenly over the pizza base. Sprinkle with the herbs, if using. Bake in a preheated 400°F oven for 30 minutes. Serve immediately.

Makes one 9 inch pizza

NOTE: As a variation, replace the green pepper with $\frac{1}{4}$ lb sliced mushrooms. Sauté the mushrooms lightly in the butter, before mixing with the pepperoni.

Savory Quiche

BASIC PIE CRUST:

1½ cups all-purpose
  flour
½ teaspoon salt
3 tablespoons butter
  or margarine
3 tablespoons
  shortening
2–3 tablespoons ice
  water

FILLING:

6 slices bacon, diced
1 small onion,
  thinly sliced
½ cup shredded
  Cheddar cheese
2 eggs, beaten
1 tablespoon chopped
  parsley (optional)
⅔ cup milk
salt and pepper

Prepare and chill the pie dough as
for Savory Leek Quiche (see page
60). Roll out and use to line an
8 inch quiche pan. Prick the pie shell,
line with foil and fill with rice.
Bake in a preheated 400°F oven for
10 minutes.

Meanwhile cook the bacon in a
skillet. Add the onion and sauté
until softened. Drain on paper
towels, then place in the pie shell.

Mix together the cheese, eggs,
parsley if using, milk and salt and
pepper to taste and pour over the
bacon and onion. Return to the
oven for 25 to 30 minutes or until
set. Serve hot or cold.

Serves 4 to 6

Traditional Pizza alla Napolitana

DOUGH:
- 1 1 lb loaf frozen white bread dough, or 1 1 lb pkg frozen pizza dough

TOPPING:
- 2 tablespoons olive oil
- 1 onion, chopped
- $\frac{3}{4}$ lb tomatoes, peeled and chopped
- 1 can (8 oz) tomato sauce
- 1 teaspoon sugar
- salt and pepper
- 1 clove garlic, crushed
- 1 bay leaf
- 1 teaspoon dried oregano or marjoram
- 1 pkg (4 oz) Mozzarella cheese, sliced
- 1 can (2 oz) anchovy fillets, drained
- 20 ripe olives

Thaw the dough according to the package directions and roll the dough out, or pat it out, to a 9 or 10 inch round. Place the round on a greased cookie sheet and chill in the refrigerator until ready to use.

Meanwhile, make the pizza topping. Heat the oil in a skillet, add the onion and sauté until softened. Add the tomatoes, tomato sauce, sugar, salt and pepper to taste, garlic, bay leaf and oregano. Simmer for 10 to 15 minutes or until the mixture is thickened. Cool and remove the bay leaf.

Spread the pizza base with the topping to within $\frac{3}{4}$ inch of the edge. Cover with the cheese slices, then arrange the anchovy fillets in a lattice pattern on top. Place an olive in each square.

Let rise in a warm place for 15 minutes, then bake in a preheated 425°F oven for 20 to 25 minutes. Serve hot.

Makes one 9 inch pizza

Potatoes with Cheese

½ teaspoon garlic
    salt
1½ lb potatoes, sliced
salt and pepper
grated nutmeg
2 cups shredded
    Cheddar cheese
1¼ cups milk

Butter a casserole and sprinkle with
garlic salt. Arrange a third of the
potato in the dish and season to
taste with salt, pepper and nutmeg.
Cover with a third of the cheese.
Repeat the layers until the potatoes
and cheese have been used up, then
pour the milk over the top.

Cook in a preheated 350°F oven
for 1 hour or until tender. Serve
immediately, with crusty French
bread.
Serves 6

DESSERTS

Family Fruit Salad

juice and grated rind
   of 1 lemon
2 red apples
2 bananas, peeled
1 can (8¾ oz) sliced
   peaches
1 can (8¼ oz)
   pineapple chunks
2 oranges

Pour the lemon juice into a glass
serving dish. Core and slice the
apples, slice the bananas, and add
both to the dish. Add the peaches
and pineapple with their syrup.
Remove all the skin and pith from
the oranges, cut into slices, and add
to the fruit salad with any juice.
Mix the fruits together thoroughly
and sprinkle with the lemon rind.
Chill for at least 1 hour before
serving.
Serves 6

Banana Splits

4 bananas
juice of $\frac{1}{2}$ lemon
3 squares (3 oz)
    semi-sweet
    chocolate,
    coarsely grated
TOPPING:
whipped cream or
    ice cream
chopped walnuts
    (optional)

Peel the bananas and split
lengthwise without cutting
through. Sprinkle with lemon juice.
Spoon the grated chocolate into the
banana splits. Wrap each banana
separately in foil and place on a
cookie sheet.

Cook in a preheated 350°F oven
for 20 minutes. Unwrap and serve
topped with whipped cream or ice
cream and chopped walnuts, if
desired.
Serves 4

Layered Fruit Gelatin

1 can (8¼ oz)
  pineapple chunks
1 pkg (3 oz) lemon-
  flavored gelatin
2 bananas
juice of 1 lemon
¼ lb raspberries
¼ lb cherries, pitted

Drain the pineapple, reserving the syrup. Add enough water to the syrup to make 2 cups, then use to make the gelatin following package instructions.

Slice the bananas and sprinkle with the lemon juice. Set aside with the pineapple, raspberries and cherries.

Pour about 1 inch of the gelatin into a dampened mold (or individual molds) and arrange the bananas in the gelatin. Allow to set, then add another layer of gelatin, and arrange another layer of fruit in this.

Repeat the layers until all the ingredients are used up, being sure to allow the gelatin to set each time. When the gelatin is completely set, unmold onto a serving dish.
Serves 6

Fluffy Orange Pudding

juice and grated rind
  of 1 orange
4 tablespoons butter
  or margarine,
  softened
½ cup sugar
1¼ cups milk
½ cup self-rising
  flour
2 eggs, separated

Put all the ingredients, except the egg whites, into a blender or food processor and process until smooth.

Alternatively, put the orange juice and rind, butter and sugar in a bowl and beat until light and fluffy, then gradually stir in the milk. Beat in the flour and egg yolks. Beat the egg whites until stiff, then fold into the mixture.

Turn into a greased 1 quart ovenproof dish and place in a pan containing enough water to come halfway up the sides of the dish.

Cook in a preheated 375°F oven for 50 minutes.
Serves 4

Raspberry Fool

1 pkg (3 oz) egg
  custard mix
1 pkg (10 oz)
  frozen
  raspberries,
  slightly thawed
½ cup heavy cream,
  whipped

Prepare the custard mix according
to package directions. Allow to cool.

Drain the raspberries, reserving
the syrup and a few raspberries for
decoration. Process the rest in a
blender or food processor, adding a
little of the syrup if necessary. Fold
in the custard and whipped cream.

Pour into 4 serving dishes and
top with the reserved raspberries.
Chill before serving.
Serves 4

Baked Apples

4 medium-size tart
  apples
1 teaspoon ground
  cinnamon
2 tablespoons butter
  or margarine
¼ cup sifted
  confectioners
  sugar
1 egg yolk
½ cup ground
  almonds
grated rind of 1
  orange
3 tablespoons brown
  sugar
4 tablespoons water

Core the apples, then make a cut in
the skin around the middle. Stand
them in an ovenproof dish and
sprinkle cinnamon around the inside
of the core cavities.

Cream together the butter,
confectioners sugar, egg yolk,
almonds and orange rind and spoon
into the apples. Top with brown
sugar.

Pour the water into the dish, then
bake in a preheated 350°F oven for
45 minutes to 1 hour until the
apples are tender.

Serves 4

Queen Pudding

1½ cups soft bread
    crumbs
2 cups milk
3 tablespoons butter
    or margarine
2 egg yolks
¾ cup sugar
grated rind of 1
    lemon
3 tablespoons jam
3 egg whites

Sprinkle the bread crumbs evenly in a 1½ quart casserole.

Heat the milk and butter until just warm. Beat the egg yolks with half the sugar. Add the lemon rind and pour on the warmed milk, stirring well. Pour this custard over the bread crumbs and bake in a preheated 350°F oven for 25 minutes or until just set.

Warm the jam and spread it over the pudding. Whisk the egg whites until stiff and fold in the remaining sugar. Pile the meringue on top of the jam and return to the oven for a further 10 to 15 minutes until the meringue is crisp and golden brown on top. Serve hot or cold.

Serves 4

Rhubarb and Apple Cobbler

1 lb rhubarb,
  chopped
1 lb tart apples,
  peeled, cored and
  sliced
½ cup sugar
1 teaspoon ground
  cinnamon
1½ cups self-rising
  flour
4 tablespoons butter
  or margarine
½ cup milk
  (approximately)

Put the prepared fruit in a saucepan with just enough water to cover the bottom of the pan. Add half the sugar and simmer for about 15 minutes until tender. Stir in the cinnamon and transfer to a casserole.

Sift the flour into a mixing bowl and rub in the butter until the mixture resembles crumbs. Add the remaining sugar, then stir in enough milk, a little at a time, to give a fairly soft dough.

Turn onto a lightly floured board and pat out to ½ inch thickness. Cut into 1½ inch rounds, using a cookie cutter, and arrange evenly around the edge of the fruit.

Brush the rounds with a little milk and bake in a preheated 400°F oven for 15 to 20 minutes or until the topping is firm and golden brown. Serve immediately.
Serves 4

Peach and Rice Meringue

1 can (16 oz) rice
  pudding
4 medium-size
  peaches, peeled
  and sliced, or 1
  can (16 oz) sliced
  peaches, drained
4 tablespoons red
  currant jelly
juice of $\frac{1}{2}$ small
  lemon
MERINGUE:
2 egg whites
6 tablespoons sugar

Pour the rice pudding into a casserole and arrange the peach slices on top. Gently warm the red currant jelly with the lemon juice, then pour over the peaches.

Whisk the egg whites until stiff, whisk in half the sugar, then fold in the rest. Spoon the meringue over the fruit and place in a preheated 350°F oven for 15 to 20 minutes until crisp and golden. Serve hot or cold.

Serves 6

Ginger Layer Dessert

3 cans (about 8½ oz
    each) sliced
    peaches,
    mandarin oranges
    or sliced pears, or
    a mixture of these
    fruits
2 cups crumbled
    gingersnaps
1½ cups heavy
    cream, whipped
chocolate sprinkles
    for decoration

Drain the cans of fruit, reserving
the syrup. Place ⅔ cup gingersnaps
in a layer in the bottom of a 1½
quart soufflé dish and spoon over
just enough of the fruit syrup to
moisten the biscuits. Arrange one
third of the fruit on top and cover
with a layer of cream.

Repeat the layers twice and chill
in the refrigerator for a few hours.
Decorate with chocolate sprinkles
before serving.
Serves 4 to 6

Pears with Chocolate Sauce

8 peeled fresh, or
    canned pear
    halves
4 squares (4 oz)
    semi-sweet
    chocolate, chopped
1 tablespoon butter
2 tablespoons corn
    syrup
2 tablespoons milk
TOPPING:
whipped cream
chopped walnuts

Arrange the pear halves in 4
individual serving dishes. Place the
chocolate in the top of a double
boiler over simmering water and
add the butter and corn syrup.
When melted, stir in the milk. Pour
the sauce over the pears, allow to
cool, then top with cream. Sprinkle
with chopped walnuts.
Serves 4

Ginger Gooseberry Pudding

1 can (16 oz)
    gooseberries
2 teaspoons ground
    ginger
6 tablespoons butter
    or margarine,
    softened
6 tablespoons sugar
1 egg, beaten
1 cup self-rising
    flour
1–2 tablespoons
    milk

Drain the gooseberries, reserving
the syrup. Place the gooseberries in
a greased casserole, pour 2
tablespoons of the syrup over them
and sprinkle with half the ginger.

Place the butter, sugar, egg,
flour, milk and remaining ginger in
a bowl and beat for 2 to 3 minutes
until smooth. Spoon over the fruit.

Bake in a preheated 350°F oven
for 45 minutes. Warm remaining
syrup and serve with the pudding.
Serves 4

Bread Pudding

2 eggs, beaten
2 cups milk
½ cup firmly packed
 brown sugar
1 teaspoon vanilla
1 teaspoon ground
 cinnamon
¼ teaspoon salt
2 cups slightly stale
 cubed bread
1 cup dried mixed
 fruit

Combine the beaten eggs, milk, brown sugar, vanilla, cinnamon and salt in a large mixing bowl. Stir well to combine.

Add the bread cubes and mix thoroughly. Stir in the dried mixed fruit.

Pour the mixture into a well greased 2 quart casserole. Bake in a preheated 350°F oven for 30 to 40 minutes until firm to the touch and golden. Serve hot, with plain or whipped cream.

Serves 6

NOTE: Leftover bread pudding is delicious served cold, next day, with whipped cream. It can also be reheated in the oven.

Apple and Date Steamed Pudding

1 cup self-rising
   flour
1 cup soft white
   bread crumbs
pinch of salt
$\frac{3}{4}$ cup shortening
2 tablespoons sugar
1 large apple,
   peeled, cored and
   finely chopped
$\frac{3}{4}$ cup chopped dates
grated rind of 1
   lemon
$\frac{1}{2}$–$\frac{3}{4}$ cup milk

Mix together the flour, bread
crumbs, salt, shortening and sugar.
Stir in the apple, dates and lemon
rind. Make a well in the center and
add enough milk to make a moist
batter. Spoon into a greased 5 to 6
cup heatproof mixing bowl with a
rim. Cover with greased foil,
pleated down the center, and tie
with string.

Place on a rack in a large saucepan. Pour in enough boiling water
to come halfway up the side of the
bowl. Cover and cook for 1$\frac{1}{2}$ to 2
hours, adding water if necessary.

Remove the foil and invert the
pudding onto a warmed serving
platter. Serve with custard.
Serves 6

Apple Meringue

1½ lb cooking
  apples, peeled,
  cored and sliced
¾ cup granulated
  sugar
  (approximately)
1 jelly roll cake,
  sliced
grated rind and juice
  of 1 lemon
2 egg whites

Put the apples in a saucepan with a little water and ¼ cup of the sugar. Bring to a boil and simmer for about 15 minutes or until soft. Process in a blender or food processor. Taste and add more sugar if necessary.

Line the bottom of a 2 quart soufflé dish with the cake slices. Spoon the lemon rind and juice over. Spread the apple purée over the top.

Whisk the egg whites until stiff. Beat in ¼ cup sugar, then fold in the remaining ¼ cup sugar.

Pile the meringue over the apple. Bake in a preheated 300°F oven for 30 minutes until the meringue is golden. Serve hot.

Serves 4 to 6

Plum Tart

BASIC PIE CRUST:
1½ cups all-purpose
  flour
½ teaspoon salt
3 tablespoons butter
  or margarine
3 tablespoons
  shortening
2 tablespoons sugar
2–3 tablespoons ice
  water
FILLING:
1 tablespoon plain
  bread crumbs
1 can (16 oz) whole
  purple plums,
  halved and pitted
¼ cup firmly packed
  brown sugar
½ teaspoon ground
  cinnamon
¼ cup sliced almonds

Prepare and chill the pie dough as for Savory Leek Quiche (see page 60), adding the 2 tablespoons of sugar before the water.

Roll out the pie dough and use to line an 8 inch quiche pan. Prick the pie shell, line with foil and fill with rice. Bake in a preheated 400°F oven for 10 minutes.

Sprinkle the bread crumbs in the baked pie crust and arrange the plum halves on top, cut side down, overlapping if necessary.

Mix together the sugar, cinnamon and almonds, and sprinkle over the plums.

Bake in a preheated 425°F oven for 40 minutes. Serve hot or cold, with cream.

Makes one 8 inch tart

78

Chocolate and Pineapple Upside-Down Cake

1 can (8¼ oz)
  pineapple slices
⅓ cup firmly packed
  brown sugar
½ cup butter or
  margarine
½ cup granulated
  sugar
2 eggs
1 cup self-rising
  flour
¼ cup Dutch-process
  cocoa

Drain the pineapple slices, reserving 2 tablespoons of the syrup. Grease an 8 inch round cake pan and line the bottom. Scatter the brown sugar in the bottom of the pan and arrange the pineapple slices on top.

Cream the butter and granulated sugar until fluffy. Beat in the eggs, one at a time. Sift the flour and cocoa together and fold into the butter mixture, alternately with the reserved pineapple syrup.

Spread the batter evenly over the pineapple slices and bake in a preheated 350°F oven for 45 to 50 minutes. Immediately invert onto a serving platter and peel off paper. Serve warm with whipped cream.

Serves 6 to 8

BAKING

Meringues

2 large egg whites
$\frac{1}{2}$ cup sugar
$\frac{3}{4}$ cup heavy cream,
whipped with 1
tablespoon sugar

Put the egg whites in a large mixing bowl and whisk until stiff. Whisk in 2 tablespoons of the sugar. Fold in the remaining sugar.

Put the mixture into a pastry bag fitted with $\frac{1}{2}$ inch plain tip and pipe 16 rounds on a cookie sheet lined with greased waxed paper or parchment.

Bake in a preheated 225°F oven for about 3 hours or until the meringues are firm to the touch. Let stand on the cookie sheet until completely cold.

Sandwich the meringues together in pairs with whipped cream just before serving.
Makes 8

Cocoa Cookies

½ cup butter or
   margarine
¼ cup sugar
1¼ cups all-purpose
   flour
1 tablespoon Dutch-
   process cocoa

Cream together the butter and
sugar, then sift the flour and cocoa
and stir into the creamed mixture.
Roll the mixture into small balls
and place well apart on greased
cookie sheets. Flatten the balls
slightly.

    Bake in a preheated 325°F oven
for 30 minutes. Let stand on the
cookie sheets for a few minutes,
then transfer to a wire rack to cool.
Makes about 20

Jam Faces

½ lb butter or
  margarine
1 cup sugar
2 eggs, beaten
⅛ teaspoon vanilla
4 cups all-purpose
  flour, sifted
strawberry jam

Cream together the butter and
sugar, then gradually beat in the
eggs and vanilla. Stir in the flour
and mix to a fairly soft dough.

Turn onto a lightly floured board
and knead gently. Roll out to about
⅛ inch thickness and cut into rounds
with a 2½ inch cookie cutter. From
half of these, remove two rounds to
represent eyes, using a ½ inch cutter,
then make a slit for the mouth.

Place all the cookies on greased
cookie sheets and bake in a
preheated 375°F oven for about 15
minutes or until golden brown. Let
stand on the cookie sheets for a few
minutes, then transfer to a wire rack
to cool.

When cold, spread the whole
cookies with jam and put the faces
on top.

Makes about 20

Shortbread

1¼ cups all-purpose
flour
pinch of salt
1 teaspoon ground
cinnamon
¼ cup sugar
¼ cup ground rice
½ cup butter, chilled
sugar for sprinkling

Sift the flour, salt and cinnamon
into a mixing bowl. Stir in the
sugar and rice. Cut in the butter
until the mixture resembles coarse
crumbs. Knead until smooth but
not sticky. Wrap in foil and chill in
the refrigerator for 30 minutes.

Press the dough out to a 7 inch
round and place on a greased cookie
sheet. Flute the edge and prick all
over with a fork. Mark into 8
portions and chill for 30 minutes.

Bake in a preheated 325°F oven
for about 40 minutes or until pale
golden. Let stand on the cookie
sheet for 10 minutes, then transfer
to a wire rack to cool completely.
Sprinkle with sugar and break the
shortbread into portions to serve.
Makes 8

Moist Fruit Cake

1 cup raisins
1 cup seeded muscats
1 cup currants
1⅓ cups firmly
    packed brown
    sugar
½ teaspoon ground
    cinnamon
½ teaspoon ground
    ginger
¾ cup butter or
    margarine
1 cup water
3 eggs, beaten
1¼ cups all-purpose
    flour
1¼ cups self-rising
    flour
½ teaspoon baking
    soda
¼ cup chopped glacé
    cherries
⅓ cup diced candied
    citrus peel
½ cup chopped
    walnuts

Put the raisins, muscats, currants, sugar, spices and butter in a saucepan with the water. Bring to a boil, stirring. Simmer for 3 minutes, then set aside to cool. When cold, stir in the eggs.

Sift the flours and baking soda into a mixing bowl and stir in the cherries, citrus peel and nuts. Stir in the fruit and egg mixture until thoroughly mixed, then turn into a lined and greased 9 inch springform pan.

Bake in a preheated 325°F oven for 1½ to 1¾ hours. Turn out and cool on a wire rack.
Makes one 9 inch cake

No-Bake Chocolate Cake

½ cup butter
2 bars (4 oz each)
    sweet baking
    chocolate
2 tablespoons corn
    syrup
2 cups cookie crumbs
¼ cup chopped glacé
    cherries
¼ cup chopped dates
½ cup shredded
    coconut

Melt the butter and chocolate in a saucepan with the corn syrup. Stir in the cookie crumbs, cherries, dates and coconut. Spoon into a greased 11 × 7 inch baking pan and press down firmly. Allow to set, then cut into squares.
Makes 32 squares

Victoria Layer Cake

½ cup butter or
    margarine,
    softened
1¼ cups sugar
1 teaspoon vanilla
3 eggs
2 cups all-purpose
    flour
1 tablespoon baking
    powder
½ teaspoon salt
1 cup milk
FILLING AND
    TOPPING:
strawberry jam or
    buttercream (see
    Butterfly Cakes)
thin slices
    crystallized lemon
    to decorate
    (optional)

Place all the cake ingredients in a
large mixing bowl and beat on
high speed for 2 to 3 minutes or
until smooth. Divide the batter
between two greased and floured 8
inch layer cake pans.

Bake in a preheated 350°F oven
for 30 to 35 minutes or until a
toothpick inserted in the center
comes out clean. Invert onto a wire
rack to cool.

Spread jam or buttercream
between the cake layers. Frost
with buttercream and decorate the
top with lemon slices, if desired.

Makes one 8 inch layer cake

VARIATIONS: Add one of the
following to the basic ingredients: ¼
cup unsweetened cocoa dissolved in
1 tablespoon hot water; or 2
teaspoons instant coffee dissolved in
1 tablespoon hot water.

Butterfly Cakes

batter for Victoria
    Layer Cake,
    plain, chocolate
    or coffee-flavored
    (see opposite
    page)
BUTTERCREAM:
6 tablespoons butter,
    softened
3 cups confectioners
    sugar, sifted
1½–2 tablespoons
    milk
1 teaspoon flavoring
    (see note)
confectioners sugar
    for sprinkling
    (optional)

Grease or line muffin pans with
paper cases and half-fill with batter.
Bake in a preheated 375°F oven for
15 to 18 minutes or until done.
Transfer to a wire rack to cool.

To make the buttercream, beat
the butter, sugar and milk together
until very smooth. Stir in the
flavoring.

Cut a slice off the top of each
cake and pipe or spoon in a little
buttercream. Cut the slices in half
and place on the cakes to resemble
butterfly wings. Sprinkle with
confectioners sugar, if desired.

Makes 18

NOTE: Flavor the buttercream with
any of the following:
1 teaspoon vanilla
1 teaspoon almond extract
1 teaspoon instant coffee dissolved
in a little hot water

Honey Gingerbread

2 cups all-purpose
  flour
½ teaspoon baking
  soda
½ cup honey
½ cup molasses
¼ cup dark corn
  syrup
¼ cup firmly packed
  brown sugar
½ cup butter or
  margarine
1 tablespoon ground
  ginger
1 teaspoon ground
  cinnamon
½ cup milk
2 eggs, beaten
chopped nuts to
  decorate
  (optional)

Sift the flour and baking soda into a bowl and make a well in the center.

Place the honey, molasses, corn syrup, brown sugar, butter, ginger, cinnamon and milk in a saucepan and heat gently, stirring constantly, until well combined. Let cool. Add the eggs and stir well. Pour into the flour mixture and beat well.

Pour the batter into a greased and floured 8 inch square pan. Sprinkle the top with chopped nuts if desired. Bake in a preheated 325°F oven for 1¼ to 1½ hours. Invert onto a wire rack and let cool.

Makes one 8 inch cake

Banana Teabread

½ cup butter or
  margarine
½ cup granulated
  sugar
¼ cup firmly packed
  brown sugar
2 eggs
2 large ripe
  bananas, mashed
2 cups self-rising
  flour
½ teaspoon baking
  soda
½ teaspoon ground
  cinnamon
¼ teaspoon grated
  nutmeg

Cream the butter and sugars together. Add the eggs, one at time, beating well after each addition. Stir in the bananas. Sift the flour, baking soda, cinnamon and nutmeg and fold into the banana mixture.

Pour into a greased 9 × 5 × 3 inch loaf pan and bake in a preheated 350°F oven for 1 hour. Remove from the pan and allow to cool on a wire rack.

Wrap the bread in plastic wrap and store overnight to enhance flavor. Slice and serve with butter.

Makes one loaf

Date and Walnut Teabread

2 cups all-purpose
 flour
1 teaspoon baking
 soda
1 teaspoon pumpkin
 pie spice
$\frac{1}{3}$ cup chopped
 walnuts
$\frac{1}{2}$ cup chopped dates
$\frac{1}{2}$ cup milk
$\frac{1}{2}$ cup firmly packed
 brown sugar
1 egg, beaten

Sift the flour, baking soda and spice together. Stir in the walnuts and dates. Place the milk and brown sugar in a saucepan. Heat gently, stirring constantly, until the sugar dissolves. Let cool slightly. Add the egg and stir well. Pour into the flour mixture and stir well.

Spread the batter in a greased 7 × 3 × 2 inch loaf pan and bake in a preheated 325°F oven for 1 hour to 1 hour 10 minutes. Remove from the pan and cool on a wire rack.
Makes one loaf

Farmhouse Bread

1 pkg (¼ oz) active
    dry yeast or 1
    cake (0.6 oz)
    compressed yeast
2 cups warm water
6–7 cups all-
    purpose flour
1½ teaspoons salt
2 tablespoons butter

Dissolve the yeast with one third of the water.

Sift the flour and salt into a large bowl and cut in the butter. Make a well in the center and pour in the yeast liquid plus the remaining water. Mix well and work with one hand until the dough comes away from the sides of the bowl.

Turn onto a lightly floured suface and knead for 10 minutes or until the dough is smooth and elastic. Place in a well greased bowl and turn to coat. Cover and let rise in a warm draft-free place until doubled in bulk.

Punch down and turn onto a floured surface; knead for 2 to 3 minutes. Divide the dough in half and place in 2 greased 9 × 5 × 3 inch loaf pans. Make a deep slash along each loaf. Cover and let rise until the dough reaches the top of the pans.

Bake in a preheated 400°F oven for 40 minutes or until the bread has shrunk from the sides of the pans and sounds hollow when tapped on the bottom. Invert onto a wire rack to cool.

Makes two loaves

Crusty Rolls

1 pkg (¼ oz) active
    dry yeast or 1
    cake (0.6 oz)
    compressed yeast
2 cups warm water
6–7 cups all-
    purpose flour
1½ teaspoons salt
1 tablespoon butter
milk to glaze

Make the dough and let rise once (as above). Punch down and knead for 2 to 3 minutes, then divide into 18 pieces. Shape into rounds and place 1 inch apart on floured cookie sheets. Cover and let rise until the rounds have doubled in size.

Brush with a little milk and bake in a preheated 450°F oven for 20 minutes. Transfer to a wire rack to cool.

Makes 18

Whole Wheat Bread

2 pkgs ($\frac{1}{4}$ oz each)
  active dry yeast
  or 2 cakes
  (0.6 oz each)
  compressed yeast
3 cups warm water
5 cups all-purpose
  flour
3 cups whole wheat
  flour
1 tablespoon salt
3 tablespoons sugar
3 tablespoons butter
TOPPING:
lightly salted water
cornflake crumbs

Make the dough as for Farmhouse
bread (see opposite), combining the
flours and stirring the sugar into the
flour mixture before adding the yeast.

Turn onto a lightly floured
surface and knead for 10 minutes,
then divide the dough in half. Place
in 2 greased and floured 9 × 5 × 3
inch loaf pans. Cover and let rise in
a warm draft-free place for about
30 minutes until doubled in bulk.
Brush with salted water and
sprinkle with cornflakes.

Bake in a preheated 400°F oven
for 1 hour or until the loaves have
shrunk from the sides of the pan
and sound hollow when tapped on
the bottom. Invert onto a wire rack
to cool.
Makes two loaves

Raisin Biscuits

2 cups self-rising
  flour
½ teaspoon baking
  powder
4 tablespoons butter
  or margarine
2 tablespoons
  sugar
¾ cup raisins
¾ cup milk
  (approximately)

Sift the flour and baking powder
into a bowl. Cut in the butter until
the mixture resembles coarse
crumbs, then stir in the sugar and
raisins. Add enough milk to make a
fairly soft dough.

Turn onto a lightly floured
surface, knead very gently, then roll
out to a ¾ inch thickness. Cut into
2 inch rounds with a fluted cutter and
place on a lightly floured cookie
sheet. Brush with milk and bake in
a preheated 425°F oven for
10 minutes. Cool on a wire rack.

Cut in half and spread with
butter and jam to serve.
Makes 10 to 12